FOR DAN,

YOU ARE MORE THAN YOUR BODY!

7 STEPS TO
HEALING BODY, MIND AND SPIRIT

by Viviane Carson M.A., D.C.H., Ph.D.

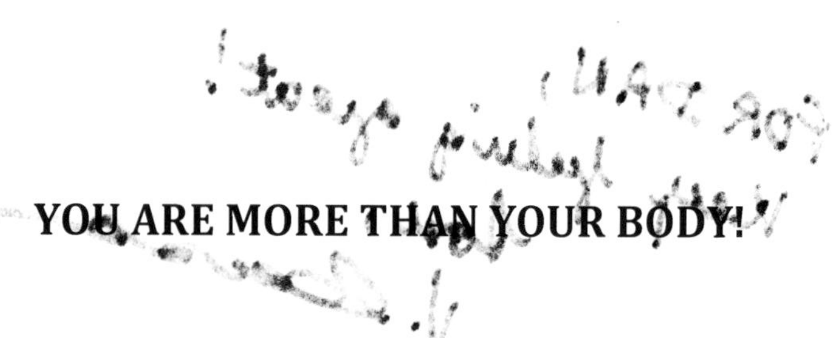

YOU ARE MORE THAN YOUR BODY!

7 STEPS TO
HEALING BODY, MIND AND SPIRIT

By Viviane Carson M.A., D.C.H., Ph.D.

ISBN 978-0-9889524-0-9

Cover photo by the author.

Printed in USA by 48HrBooks

This book is dedicated to:

My patients who will always have a place in my heart.

REVIEWS FROM PATIENTS WHO WERE TREATED BY DR. VIVIANE CARSON:

(The following testimonials are unedited and were written in a signed release. Some names have been changed to protect the identity of the person.)

From the day I walked into your office, I was full of anxiety. I didn't think I could get over the depression, or get what I wanted in my life. After the 3rd session, I completely got rid of all my doubts and got rid of all old patterns. I was able to find love and I got work. You were absolutely right about everything! I still use all the tools you gave me. You inspired me. I would like to tell everyone to do all 3 sessions. You gave me strength to move on in my life. I found peace. It was all worth it! I wish more people would find it! Thanks for giving me my life back! Thank you for all your efforts and your time, Dr. Carson.

~ Marian

I was at my breaking point and called Dr. Carson's office to make an appointment. After meeting with Dr. Carson, I am calm, I deal with negative issues by letting them go, not dwelling on them. I feel like a new, improved and refreshed person. I am just very grateful for everything you've done for me!

~ Kathy

Before meeting with Dr. Carson, I had such extreme anxiety, feeling I had no hope for a better life. After going through treatment with Dr. Carson, I feel happy, relaxed, and I have a great future ahead of me ANXIETY FREE. Thank you Dr. Carson so much for helping me to get my life back and for helping people get out of their bondage and leading them to freedom.

~ Christine

I came here to get rid of my anxiety and panic symptoms and the frustrating and terrifying lies they brought me... Now, I have a better outlook as the person I truly am. I feel that I have gotten rid of the guilt and anger and stress and physical pain and everything that had brought my life to misery, and can move forward and live a normal and happy life.

~ Scott

I needed help with my anxiety and panic attacks. I feel I have received the help that I searched for, for a very long time. I feel strong enough so that I don't have the need for medications. I also lost weight and feel confident that I will continue to lose weight. I have also felt a healing in my soul of so many open wounds that I tried to cover up since childhood. Thank you so much Dr. Carson. You're the greatest!

~ America

Dr. Carson helped me learn to deal with stress and remove negative thoughts. I came to her really stressed out and had a tightness in my chest from the stress. The first session, Dr. Carson taught me how to relax and gave me tools to help me control my subconscious mind from thinking negative and help me "let it go" so that I would not get stressed out. The next day, the pain in my chest was gone for good and my stress level was lower. During the second session, Dr. Carson gave me another tool to prevent stress from building up. It works great. After the final session, my treatment is complete and I feel like I am really in charge of my life. Thanks Dr. Carson.

~ Mark

I don't have panicky, depressive thoughts or feel sick to my stomach anymore. I also don't feel like I need to smoke cigarettes. This therapy has helped me overcome negative thoughts that made me feel mentally and physically unwell for some years. I have had definite results from this therapy that I have not received elsewhere, more than years of therapy.

~ Elizabeth

I saw Dr. Carson for weight. After the first session, the weight began to shift so that my clothes were looser. I was also treated for anxiety and depression. Both are gone. And the pain in my knee is also completely gone! I feel so much better, I won't need the surgery I was scheduled for!

~ Annie

When I first came in I was afraid to leave my house, missed out on important events and parties with my kids. I can leave my house without feeling fear or anxiety and I'm now returning to class. Thank you for helping me get my life back.

~ Keisha

Depression is gone, I am able to sleep better, healed anger and anxiety. I have better self-awareness. Also healed my bladder. I love you, Dr. Carson!

~ Angela

Looking at him when he first came in, Dionze was a mess! Now, after three treatments, he is happy and peaceful. He's a normal kid now. His energy is positive and he's learned how to express himself. He's not angry anymore. He's confident. Now he can have a normal childhood: calm, the depression is gone, the fear is gone, and most important, the asthma is gone. Dionze has found peace within himself. No more nightmares, so he can sleep now. Thank you Dr. Carson.

~ Mother of Dionze,
8 years old

Dr. Carson provided me with the necessary tools to heal my intense fight/flight response, anger, guilt, and depression which came from experiencing child abuse from an alcoholic father, and, later, 11 years of spousal abuse. My life is calmer on a daily basis and others are noticing and remarking about that. I wish I hadn't waited so long to get help and wish I'd found her sooner.

~ Lucy

When I first came to see you, Dr. Carson, I was in a very bad way. I couldn't sleep at all, couldn't speak, stayed home most of the time. Now, I fall asleep easily with your tools, and since you helped me with the PTSD, my nightmares are gone. You did good for me.

~ Guy

Dr. Viviane helped me heal from PTSD from 55 years ago that had affected my life on a professional and personal level. Most recently becoming a widow and experiencing new relationships. Now I can go forward in life happy and complete.

~ Linda

I wanted to come and see Dr. Carson initially as a last resort. I had been through many standard psychotherapies and none of them worked. As soon as I met Dr. Carson, I knew I would be helped. I was home. In four wonderful sessions. I truly no longer suffer from crippling depression, anxiety, sadness, guilt and shame. I was cured of lifelong PTSD. Dr. Carson's wisdom and revolutionary techniques helped me accomplish all my goals. I believe Dr. Carson has a gift for helping others.

~ Cat

I am healed from diabetes, stress, insomnia, anxiety and depression. I sleep much better. My blood pressure is down and I feel so good. Thank you, Dr. Carson.

~ Milagros

When I first came in, I wasn't sure how this would work, but I was tired of the constant pain. I was willing to try and it proved to be a great experience for me. All the pains in my lower back were removed. I am not worrying anymore about being young with a painful back problem for the rest of my life. I feel much better about myself and my stress level is lower than it has ever been.

~ John

Dr. Carson, you helped me tremendously. I'm sleeping every night. Things are so good - uterus/cervix - no cancer anymore. You helped me to take care of me and let God. I know God spoke to me through you. I think what you do is commendable! It's not easy. Thanks.

~ Sherry

After suffering for more than 3 decades with seizures, stress, accidents and emotional pain, I can finally see the light... a new beginning. My cure is not with drugs, but healing by mending emotions of the mind and heart. Things you would never imagine to be the cause of your illness will completely surprise you. I think it is nearly impossible to find a cure by your self without professional help. I'm so glad I found Dr. Viviane Carson. She helped me to find the cause of my seizures and showed me how I can remove the seizures from my life forever. The power of the mind is amazing. The power of positive energy and believing you can help your body heal itself is what Dr. Carson has helped me to understand. I know she can help others the way she helped me. Thank you so much.

~ Sara

We are not human
beings having a spiritual experience.
We are spiritual beings having a human experience.

Pierre Teilhard de Chardin

ABOUT THE AUTHOR

Dr. Viviane Carson has seven degrees, including two doctorates, and certification in 17 sub-modalities. She has over 30 years of experience in leading personal growth workshops and seminars and one-on-one counseling. Dr. Viviane has developed a unique methodology she calls "Psychobiophysical Healing"™ to effectively empower clients to achieve mental, emotional, physiological and biochemical changes very quickly. As a Doctor of Clinical Hypnotherapy, she uses a combination of relaxation-training techniques along with her healing method and has been able to help clients to heal from the root cause of most conditions, usually in three treatments.

You Are More Than Your Body! leads readers to the root causes which are at the base of most illnesses. The methods outlined here are alternative/holistic and complementary to conventional medical treatment. Dr. Viviane is not a physician, and encourages you to seek medical advice from your own doctor, continue to treat any illnesses, and continue to take any medications that have been prescribed by a physician.

For classes and training for certification, more information is available at: http://www.drvcarson.com or call (661) 266-9696.

TABLE OF CONTENTS

FOREWORD

Everything begins at the level of Mind. You are not your body: you're so much more than just your body. You are a magnificent creation capable of re-creating your health, and reclaiming your birthright of being healthy and happy and free!

What if you could learn how to use your mind in such a way that you could get rid of anxiety or depression, or Post Traumatic Stress Disorder, eliminate medications (with the help of your M.D.), and/or reverse a serious diagnosis? What if you could believe that you could heal any condition whether it is emotional or physiological? Or, what if you could achieve any dream, any desire? What if you could even change your past? And what if you could do any of this easily and effortlessly, using your imagination, almost like playing a game of make believe?

The answers to all these questions are in this book. This book is to be used as though you are following a course of treatments. Each chapter is to be worked on for at least a week before moving on to the next. Please do not move on until you have absorbed the information in each chapter and you are easily able to use all the tools outlined in each one for at least one week. You may find that you have to go back and redo a chapter if you are noticing that you have forgotten some of the steps.

You are not just a three-dimensional being, you are multi-dimensional, able to affect yourself on every level: mental/emotional, psychological, physiological, biochemical, spiritual, and beyond!

Thoughts are things. Thoughts have energy and power, made up of electro-magnetic frequencies. When you begin with your thinking, and you decide to change your thoughts, you will change your world. You may have already been told that everything begins with a thought.

Acknowledging your thoughts, however, is not enough to effect change. You can begin to not only recognize when you are having negative thoughts, but you can alter the whole belief system that has created the problem you are experiencing. You can also learn to change the biochemistry in your body so that you not only get rid of anxiety or depression or anger, but also most physiological illnesses or dis-eases, and change your past, so that you can even alter your DNA!!!

This may sound far-fetched, but hundreds of people have healed by following the program I have outlined for them because this approach does work.

I noticed this in my own life when I was taking stock of the events that led me to wanting to help others. When I was four years old, I was left behind during a revolution that was happening where I lived at the time, in Cairo, where my Dad had an import-export firm. We were told to evacuate our building as the Arabs were fire-bombing British banks and we happened to live above one. As we came out of the building, I was separated from my Mom, Dad, and Grandma, and ended up standing alone, paralyzed with fear, as I watched the bank across the lane going up in flames, seeing the people inside burning. I remember the foul smell of burning flesh, the chaos of men in white robes completely out of control, the screaming, a huge bonfire in the middle of the street fed by looted furniture, and wondering if I, too, would end up in the middle of the conflagration. I also remember the relief I felt when I spotted one black face in the sea of coffee ones: our servant, Bekhit, who was also my friend and savior, plucking me out of the inferno to carry me to safety where the rest of the family was waiting. (1)

This trauma stayed in all the cells of my body for many years until I was able to begin to talk about it in therapy, but no matter how many times I recalled this incident out loud, it would still haunt me and prevent me from being in crowd celebrations and family picnics without feeling the panic again and again.

I knew that this trauma was locked in my cells and became a cellular memory because anything to do with crowds would trigger fear, or anger, or the need to run away. This is what's called a "fight or flight response" which is part of our automatic brain mechanism and which when triggered often in childhood, can cause a series of reactions which create a "hijacking" of the brain into fear, anger and even rage. (2)

As a teenager, I knew I wanted to study psychology so that I could help myself and others overcome these fears. I eventually became a psychologist and learned that although I understood the cause and effect relationship of trauma, talking about it over and over or having my clients talk about it over and over was not healing anyone. So, I studied the brain in an effort to understand the mechanics of these triggers, but at the time, there was no research to support what I began to notice in my work.

At first, it was trial and error, but eventually, I was able to develop a way of working with people that helped them to heal from the root cause. I call my methodology, "Psychobiophysical Healing"™ and it has yielded a 100% success rate over the last seventeen years, not just for emotional conditions, but with most physiological ailments as well for those who followed directions, completed treatment in a timely manner and used the tools I give them to empower them. (3)

This book is not meant to substitute treatment in my healing center, but can be used either in addition to or as a part of your regular conventional medical treatment. Always consult your primary physician first, in order to get a diagnosis, course of treatment and prognosis. In my center, I devise a treatment program based on your diagnosis, your personality, your needs, likes and dislikes, your lifestyle, and much more. I look at everything you have done to help yourself, your nutrition, your daily physical habits including any exercise regimen or lack of one, your thinking patterns, your breathing patterns, and many other factors that I pick up intuitively as an empath and from reading the deepest, unspoken patterns of your psyche. Never stop any medications prescribed to you, and again, please consult your physician if you feel that you are ready to be weaned off them. You can find more information at my website, (http://www.drvcarson.com) and read hundreds of testimonials from patients who are grateful for the healing they experienced in only three treatments. (4)

(The names of patients used in this book have been changed to protect their privacy.)

PREFACE

Most people have P.T.S.D. or Post Traumatic Stress Disorder and don't even know it.

If you think you don't have PTSD, think again.

If you have any of the following symptoms, you have PTSD:

1. Excess weight or any eating disorder.
2. Anxiety, excessive worry or obsessive thinking for any prolonged period of time.
3. Depression, "what's-the-use" kind of feelings for a prolonged period of time.
4. Grief or sorrow that you may not even be aware of (often feels like a part of you is missing) that doesn't seem to go away.
5. Anger that expresses itself towards yourself or anyone else, as well as anger held in.
6. Guilt that keeps you from putting yourself first in some situations or in most.
7. Pain, (emotional or physical) that does not go away.
8. Any illness that is persistent, whether it has been diagnosed or not.
9. Addictions of any kind - from smoking to being a workaholic.

If you have answered yes to one or more of the above questions, then you have Post Traumatic Stress Disorder and although it seems to be the root cause of most dis-ease, it is the most serious result, which, in turn, creates a series of behavioral patterns which will surprise you. The real, root cause underlies the PTSD and you will be able to find it for yourself if you follow all seven of the steps outlined.

It's been hiding in your cells for many, many years and comes from one or more childhood incidents that were negative and never addressed physiologically. PTSD is triggered when something traumatic happens but, often, looking back it doesn't always feel like trauma, or you can't remember anything or much of your childhood. Just look for the symptoms (above) and you will know that you experienced some kind of difficulty.

This does not mean that you have to relive your entire childhood. However, you can change your past. There is a way of working with your unconscious mind that will help you to even turn your past around. There is also another part of you that is within you which is inborn; and that is, your ability to become happy. Happiness is an inherent part of you, and when you learn how to externalize that part that is inherent within you, you can be happy no matter what the outside circumstances are.

There is an indomitable part of you that can help you overcome whatever is bringing you to your knees right now. You can learn how to use this part of you that can help you to overcome almost anything, and I am going to show you how.

Seven Secrets to Healing That You Will Learn In This Book:

1. Embarking on the journey to take charge of your own unconscious mind.
2. Stopping all the negative self-talk now!
3. Training your body-mind-spirit to let go and relax in a few seconds no matter what is going on around you.
4. Discovering the root cause of your anxiety, depression, and any other condition, and processing it so that you are free of trauma from your past.
5. Learning how to forgive in an effective way for you.
6. Processing the negative emotions from your past, present, and future.
7. Setting a goal for your new life, knowing that you can easily accomplish it!

We cannot solve our problems with the same thinking we used when we created them.

Albert Einstein

CHAPTER ONE

TAKE CHARGE
OF YOUR UNCONSCIOUS MIND

Before I take you step by step into the healing process, I'm going to go back in time in my own life. I didn't just wake up one day and decide that I would help people to heal. I had to first heal myself from a past that most therapists labeled as horrific.

I had no idea that my journey would take me from feeling powerless as a child and being traumatized to the point where I felt I could not speak, to becoming successful as an alternative health care practitioner helping people to heal from severe trauma as well as many different kinds of conditions.

My trauma started in the country I happened to live in as a child: Egypt. I was born into a French family and as part of a minority of whites living in a third-world country, I was exposed to persecution, revolution, killings, disappearance of people I loved, rape, and other indescribable, devastating experiences at a very early age. I have recorded the details of these events in my memoirs entitled, "Kindred Spirits" which is due to be published soon, so I will not go into my whole story here.

However, I would like to include relevant details so that I can encourage others to heal what seemed like overwhelming obstacles for me at the time. At 18 months of age, I was left alone in a hotel room by the Red Sea when something happened that caused me to begin to be afraid of being left alone after dark. It took me many years to be able to recall the details of this experience, but eventually, I was able to process the trauma of being held at knifepoint by an intruder who was frightened away by the commotion in the hallway as I cried out for help. Up until then, I was able to go off to sleep without lights in the room, but after this incident, I kept on asking for reassurance from my parents who would then comfort me by tapping lightly on my shoulder until I would fall asleep.

By age three, I was a precocious, expressive child with an extensive vocabulary, and the ability to express feelings and observations with enthusiasm. I was basically a happy child, and, although I was sensitive and insightful, I was unable to verbalize my insights to my Mom who was ill and had her own trouble dealing with a life she had not been prepared to live in a conscious way. At that time, my Dad decided to take my Mom, who had been experiencing severe back pain, to meet with the best orthopedic surgeons in France. So, instead of leaving me with my grandmother who lived with us, they decided to drop me off at an orphanage in southern France which was highly recommended in our community. This orphanage was known for taking good care of children who came from French families on a temporary basis.

So I was taken to France by my parents on a wonderful four-day cruise crossing the Mediterranean Sea from Alexandria to Marseille. And just as I was beginning to thrive in the unaccustomed attention from both my parents, I was left at the orphanage with no explanation or preparation for the separation that took place. Even though this was to be a temporary separation, I thought I had been left there permanently.

Abandonment is at the root cause of PTSD and every condition that follows. However, not all abandonment is physical. I had been abandoned emotionally by both my parents long before, who believed the trend at the time, that when a child cries, she should not be picked up and soothed or comforted. As a result, I had developed a hernia from the effort of crying so much.

Children who are left in their cribs for long periods of time can develop Failure to Thrive Syndrome which can lead to infant mortality. (I believe that even adults can suffer from FTT when they are deprived of physical and emotional affection.)

All abandonments, both emotional and physical, are major trauma which become embedded in the psyche of the child, and like an invisible wound, festers in every cell of the body. Later on, this wound surfaces as any one of the many conditions listed at the beginning and on the back of this book. This is called, "cellular memory" which will trigger a fight or flight response whenever a similar event triggers all the neurons in the brain firing in nearby associative pathways. A similar event could be being alone in an unfamiliar environment, later, as an adult.

If at any time during the traumatic event, a child is touched appropriately or inappropriately anywhere on the body, the trauma will be anchored into that area of the body, another feature of "cellular memory" which explains, in extreme cases, why children who are raped, will later, as adults, have trouble being touched even lovingly in areas not necessarily in the vicinity of the genitals. (5)

All trauma can be hidden in the unconscious mind which protects the conscious mind by releasing certain hormones that cause a form of amnesia or anesthesia, which is why many people have no memories or little memory before a certain age. These memories can be retrieved in hypnotic regressions but the clinician has to be very adept at processing the recovered memory so as not to trigger more negative reactions later. (6)

So, taking charge of your unconscious mind is the first step to taking charge of your life. If you are living your life without being in charge of your unconscious mind, you are subject to anything that comes up that can throw you off course. It's sort of like being a passenger in a car, as opposed to taking the wheel and steering your life to where you want to go.

You can benefit from over thirty years of research and development I engaged in, by following the secrets to healing that I am divulging here step by step, for the first time!

Let's make it very simple: there are only two parts to you - conscious and unconscious.

The unconscious mind is just a robot: it does everything you tell it to do. How? Through every thought you think, every word you say, and every action you take. So that's everything you think, say or do! Everything you think, say or do is a direct command to your unconscious mind. If you think a positive thought, your unconscious will deliver more positive thoughts and vice versa. What we focus on, grows. If you say one thing, but your actions are contradicting what you say or think, your unconscious, being a robot, will turn around and perform the latest command. It does not analyze, evaluate or assess the consequences. It just performs.

It takes 67 seconds of thinking a negative thought for it to appear in some form in your reality! (7)

Your unconscious works at a very primitive level and is very literal in its understanding. So because it is so literal, I do not use the word "lose" weight in my practice. Something lost, will have to be found, which may explain, in part, the resistance some people find in releasing weight!

It also, does not understand a "do not" command. "I'm not going to panic," only causes you to have an anxiety attack. Similarly, if you are thinking, "I'm not going to have another piece of cake." It hears the opposite: "I am going to have another piece of cake!" It's like a child who does exactly what you tell it not to do. (Words like don't, not and no, have the same effect on the unconscious.)

If you reframe the command into a positive one, "I know I could have another piece of cake, but I also know how lousy that feels right after I eat it. So I'll have a piece of sweet fruit instead, like some grapes."(8) However, it's not that easy to make this decision and keep it. You may find that you are contradicting your thoughts or words and actions. You may have to ask yourself, "What is it that I really need when I reach for that piece of cake? Is it comfort, love, understanding?" It is usually an unfulfilled need or a hidden emotion which has to be acknowledged before it can leave you at peace. Later, you will learn how to take care of these needs for yourself so that you can stop being self-destructive.

All this time, you've been giving yourself the wrong commands and getting the very results you're trying to avoid! So, it's best to become very mindful of the inner language or our thoughts that are negative, but doing that alone is not sufficient to turn the negatives around. Remember that even when you are focusing on a need, you are focusing on what you do not want, or the lack of what you would like to have in your life. The result is that you get what you do not want! Don't feel bad! Now you have the knowledge to do something different!

In my clinic, I usually use "Applied Kinesiology"®, a form of advanced muscle testing, to show you how every thought creates your reality, whether it's positive or negative.(9) Every thought you think either feels good or bad.

It's that simple. Each one of these thoughts is creating your future. So, if you're wondering why your life is not going in the direction you would like it to, examine your thinking patterns. Once you understand how your thinking affects your life, you will begin to live consciously, making decisions that expand your life rather than diminish it.

How will you know you've had a negative thought? Thoughts come and go at the speed of lightning. Researchers have pointed out that the average person thinks 60,000 thoughts a day, minimum! So how do we keep track of our thoughts? Through our body!

Do you ever go through a day, when sometime, usually in the afternoon, you feel tired? Or do you sometimes feel anxious or depressed or sad or irritated/angry? That's because thoughts are things. Thoughts are electro-magnetic frequencies, as supported in Quantum Physics findings,[(10)] and we are constantly bombarding others with our thoughts or we are being bombarded by someone else's thoughts. So it's not just our own thoughts we need to be mindful of, but that of others too. Do you ever go to a mall and find that pretty soon, you are uncomfortable or feel like leaving? That's because of all the negative thoughts exchanged in an enclosed area. It's easy to be thrown off track when in a positive mood because negative thoughts are denser and heavier than positive ones, and can bring us down. So you will know you have had a negative thought when you are tired in the middle of the day for no apparent reason, or feeling anxious or depressed or irritable or any other negative emotion.

Everything begins with a thought.
The point of power is in the present moment.

Louise L. Hay

CHAPTER TWO

STOP ALL THE NEGATIVE SELF-TALK NOW!

Do you know the story of the man who was driving up a winding mountain road when, suddenly, from behind a blind buff, a car appears, driving fast in the opposite direction, and a woman yells out of her window, "PIG!" The man returns the insult, by yelling back, "BITCH!", continues to drive around the corner and drives right into the pig on the road!

Don't we all make assumptions and react before we have a chance to understand what is really happening on a deeper level? This is the paradigm shift that will change how you have been seeing yourself and your world.

When you find yourself reacting negatively, that is, feeling tired, or feeling that you are on a downward cycle, or any emotions that feel out of control, like feeling overwhelmed or about to give up, you have to interrupt this pattern. You interrupt this pattern by switching to a different way of treating yourself, and by beginning to become aware of the little child within you, the part of you who is vulnerable and who was helpless that you carry everywhere with you. Begin to be kind to yourself by guiding this precious little child, by protecting this child and giving her the encouragement and love she needs to hear. We will be working with your inner child in another chapter, further along.

Now, I am about to give you your first tool. Can you accept that you have the power within you to interrupt these negative thoughts, whether they are yours or someone else's?

Here is how you interrupt the negativity. First, you give yourself the command, "Stop!" to yourself, to freeze the negative thought, just as you would yell out to that kid inside you to prevent her from stepping out into the traffic. (See Chapter 5)

Then, you give yourself another command: "Cancel!", a very powerful word in the English language which erases all the negativity that came before, during, and after the negative thought itself.

And finally, you replace the negative thought with a positive affirmation. An affirmation is a positive thought that is not yet true for us, but that we would like to be true. You can say, "I am in charge of my life now!" with conviction and authority.

Remember, your unconscious does not understand a statement worded in the negative. So there are no negative wordings in these commands. They are in the present tense, and they have a deadline. Your unconscious accepts these commands immediately and also knows when to perform them. If you state the command using the future tense, it will remain in the future and not become a part of your life in the present moment.

When you first start using this tripartite tool, you will get a lot of resistance. You'll start thinking, "Why am I doing this? No one cares. What's the use? I've tried everything. Nothing ever works." This is normal. After all, it's a law of physics, Newton's Law, that for every action, there is an equal and opposite reaction. This is why when we begin to grow and move forward, we get obstacles. This is the time to use your tool. STOP! CANCEL! I AM IN CHARGE OF MY LIFE NOW! You keep saying these words over and over again to yourself for the first 48 hours. That's how long it takes to re-pattern your brain to begin to become positive.

Your brain has been marinating in negative hormones for most of your life but if you keep repeating these three commands, you are changing the marinade by raising the serotonin levels and the dopamine levels and the endorphins begin to kick in. It's like getting a good physical workout that makes you feel euphoric.

If you stop using this tool after 48 hours and you notice that you're still having negative thoughts, it means that you have to continue the repetition.

Soon, you will begin to notice that you're already feeling better, that you're a lot more positive than you used to be. Now, you use the tool as needed. How will you know you need it? When you feel tired, or down, or fearful, or irritable or negative. Yep, you know the rest!

Eventually, you may notice that you even wake up with a smile on your face!

Sean was fifteen years old, and was accompanied by both his loving parents to my clinic. He was very tall and very skinny. His mother tearfully explained that he had stopped eating because he kept saying that every time he tried to swallow any food, he would choke and he would spit out the food and refuse to eat it. He had been checked out by several doctors who had told his parents that there was nothing physically wrong with him.

Further questioning of Sean led me to the conclusion that he had paired a negative incident in which he had been rushed to eat and had gagged, with a fear of swallowing and choking. He kept saying that he was afraid to die. His negative thoughts were his biggest enemies. So, I interrupted the negative thoughts for him first, and gave him the tool to continue to interrupt them himself.

When he came back forty-eight hours later, he already looked better and his parents told me that he was beginning to be more positive. After the next treatment, he started to eat again, and by the end of his third treatment, his parents happily reported that he was eating everything in sight, just like any other healthy teenager!

Three decades ago it was considered scientific heresy for a Harvard physician and researcher to hypothesize that stress contributed to health problems and to publish studies showing that mental focusing techniques were good for the body.

Herbert Benson

CHAPTER THREE

RELAXATION TRAINING

Now that you've stopped the negative thoughts, you can learn how to relax yourself. I'm not talking about going to a spa or getting a massage. Although that wouldn't hurt. And no, you're not going on a trip. Not in the traditional sense. But in your mind. Don't give up now! This is not woowoo stuff. This is brain technology. I'm going to teach you to take yourself on a guided meditation.

Before beginning the relaxation training, it would be best if you would rate yourself on the various issues you are treating. You could rate yourself on how often you are negative on a scale of 0 to 10, the latter being the most often. You could also rate yourself on specific emotions so that you are keeping track of your progress before you start. Rate yourself on your anxiety level, your depression level and any other emotions such as anger, guilt, grief, stress, pain (both physical and emotional). You could also keep track of what you would like to achieve; such as happiness, success, fulfillment, etc., where 0 would be none and 10 would be the best for you. Develop your own rating scales. Rate yourself at the beginning of every chapter and at the end of every chapter in this book, and notice your progression.

First, you need to pick a location out in nature that has no negative association from the past. So if you went to the beach with your ex and you had an argument there, this is not the place. You can decide to go to a place you've always wanted to go. Or you can create it in your imagination, like a quiet, peaceful meadow. It has to be a place where you feel safe and where you can relax completely and be by yourself. It can't be a place where you'll actively do something. You can ride your horse or bike or motorcycle before and/or after you've laid your body on the sand or on the grass or against a tree in the forest; but first, you pick that place where you will be still. And no, you don't have to still your mind and get rid of all your thoughts! Just follow me step by step, and I'll take you there.

So you've picked the ideal place where you know you can let go and calm down. Before you take yourself there, you are going to learn the biggest secret to creating relaxation in your body: how to breathe. Yes, I know you think you know how to breathe! You've been doing it all your life! But diaphragmatic breathing will bring more oxygen into your bloodstream, and displace any toxins you've accumulated from shallow breathing, smoking (yuck), breathing polluted air, etc.

You start by taking a deep breath in through your nose as you count to four, then you bring that breath into your abdomen, expanding it as much as you can, holding it in for another count of four, and then blowing the breath out through your mouth as if you're blowing out all the candles on your birthday cake for the last count of four. So it's four in, four held in, four out. The exhale has to be cold air. If you're breathing out hot air, as in cleaning your sunglasses, it won't work. We are replenishing your bloodstream, clearing it of toxins.

You now take one of these deep breaths as you begin to relax your body from your toes to the top of your head. Just picture the relaxation coming into your toes, breathe in for four, hold in for four, exhale for four and let your toes and feet relax. Then, move up to your ankles, doing the same breathing. In between deep breaths, breathe normally for a few seconds, or you will hyperventilate, get dizzy, and give up.

Next, move up to your lower leg muscles, and let go of all tension from the knees, down. Then, up to your thigh muscles. Remember to keep breathing through your abdomen counting to four in, four held in, four out. You got it! Next, you will do the same thing relaxing your abdomen, then your chest, your shoulders (dropping your shoulders), bringing the relaxation down your arms all the way to your fingertips. At this point, you may feel a tingling in your fingertips. That's part of the relaxation process. You may get tingling sensations in other parts of your body.

Next, you will do the breathing, bringing the relaxation into your neck breathing out any tension knots, down your spine progressively, all the way to the tip of your spine, relaxing every muscle along the way. Then, back up into your neck again but going up behind your ears and into your scalp so that every hair follicle relaxes! Onto your forehead, eyes, cheeks, mouth and chin, making sure you dropped your jaw so that even your tongue and your throat are relaxed.

Now you begin to count backwards in your mind from ten to zero, transporting yourself to your chosen place (the beach, forest, meadow, or any other place you chose) and put in all the sights, sounds, smells and sensations as you sense yourself taking one or more steps for every count backwards. Don't worry if you don't see it all clearly in your mind. This is not a movie. If you have the sensation that you are in this place, that's fine.

Ten, you're exploring. It's a beautiful day, the temperature is just perfect for you. Nine, you're slowly moving towards that area where you will lie down eventually. Keep putting in all the sights, sounds, smells, sensations. Be creative, use your imagination. With practice, it will get easier and feel better and better.

Continue counting backwards, nine, eight, seven, concentrating on the sights, sounds, smells, sensations.

At six, you've found the ideal location to lie down. At five you are lying down making sure you are completely comfortable. At four and three you have allowed your arms and legs to feel so heavy, you have a floating sensation. (Don't worry if you don't have it right away.) Two, one. At zero, you are in the most relaxed state you have ever experienced in your entire life! Release a long, deep breath.

Now think of one word that makes you feel good; such as "peaceful" or "relaxed" or "free", any one word that you will use from now on that will become your trigger word. This word will eventually be the trigger that immediately, automatically relaxes you from the tips of your toes to the top of your head and that will also, automatically bring you back to this place, which is your safe place, so that you don't have to put in all the time and effort you used the first time you relaxed yourself.

Next, you picture your new life, free from any of your old negative patterns, happy, healthy and healed. You will be doing this meditation three times a day for two to five minutes at a time, picturing the end-result of whatever you desire to accomplish. It does not have to take more than five minutes at a time after the initial training. When you feel comfortable and have pictured what you want to achieve that day, you bring yourself out of the relaxation with the words you used before: "I am in charge of my life now!" You are doing an active meditation. If you're falling asleep, you will not get the results you want.

Congratulations! You just gave yourself your first hypnosis session! Hypnosis is not something someone else does to you. It is simply a brain-wave activity that occurs whenever you are relaxed. You are not asleep, unconscious or out of it. You can hear everything going on around you, but you are more deeply relaxed. You engage in self-hypnosis anytime you are doing a repetitive task, or driving or using any electronics or relaxing in some way of your own.

From now on, when you want to go back to that state of complete relaxation, all you have to do is sit back, close your eyes, take your three deep diaphragmatic breaths, say your trigger word to yourself, and immediately, quite automatically, you are relaxed from the tips of your toes to the top of your head and you are back in your safe place where you can picture, sense and feel yourself accomplishing your goals. You do not have to go through the progressive muscle relaxation after the first time. When you can sense that you actually feel the sensation of accomplishment, you bring yourself out of the meditation. You can use the phrase you already know to bring yourself out of trance: "I am in charge of my life now!"

There has to be a willingness on your part to accept that you are ready to let go of the need to control it all, and to allow your unconscious to help you make those desires real.

Exercises when conflict comes up:

If you find that you're having trouble relaxing, letting go even after you have followed the directions outlined above, or there may be times when you are overwhelmed or preoccupied with thoughts that will not allow you to go to your safe place, you can do the following exercise:

Use your deep breathing, and refrain from forcing anything. Instead of forcing yourself to visualize your safe place, just concentrate on your breathing and imagine that the thoughts you are having are like butterflies landing on you. Observe each butterfly, and eventually, it will go on its way. You don't swat it, or tell it to go away. You look at it, and admire its beauty. It has come out of the cocoon of the caterpillar and has become a beautiful butterfly, just like you when you allow it to happen!

Another exercise you can do if you are able to get to your safe place in your imagination but find that you take yourself out of it before you can complete your visualization, just focus on one element in nature around you that feels good, such as a leaf on a tree, or a wave if you are at the beach, or a blade of grass. One element that makes you feel that "aahhhh, now I can relax" feeling and breathe through that element. Feel yourself becoming one with that element. What would it be like to be a leaf or a wave or a blade of grass?

You will find yourself letting go more easily if you use one of the two exercises above. You can also do the muscle relaxation described at the beginning of this chapter all over again, concentrating on relaxing one group of muscles at a time from your toes to the top of your head.

If you're still having trouble getting yourself relaxed, call me for an appointment!

When the imagination and will power are in conflict, are antagonistic, it is always the imagination which wins, without any exception.

Émile Coué

CHAPTER FOUR

DISCOVERING THE ROOT CAUSE OF YOUR ANXIETY, DEPRESSION, PTSD AND ANY OTHER CONDITION

Eric, a 65 year-old man was brought into my healing center by his wife Suzannah who told me that he had become impossible to get along with and that he would get angry and overreact to anything she would say, to the point of going off into rages. When I asked him to tell me what was happening for him, what he thought was getting him angry, the impression I got was that he was being stifled or even suffocated, so I asked him what had happened in his childhood that could have stifled or suffocated him. He was hesitant to answer this question, but then he started to cry, and as I encouraged him to go on simply by listening to him, the story came out.

He was born in Germany, and when he was four years old, World War II had broken out. Whenever the alarm would sound that enemy planes were beginning to drop bombs, he and his family would enter the shelter beneath his house. The shelter did not help during this particular raid. He remembered a huge explosion and then darkness as he was buried under the debris of his collapsed building. He was pulled out of the ruins of his home by his father. No one else in his family survived, and as he and his father began to leave the area, he could hear the cries of neighbors who were still buried alive.

This is a very extreme case of PTSD and had remained with him for over 60 years. Eric did not know he had PTSD. He had literally buried this trauma in his past by forgetting it, and had been mostly OK, but when his anger began to surface inexplicably for him, he had not remembered the incident. Once he remembered it in my office, I was able to process the root cause of his anger which was the actual incident itself, and he went back to being his usual jovial self after three treatments.

Other war veterans have come back with PTSD and have all (those who do come for help) recovered from the very severe symptoms they had been experiencing. However, you do not have to have survived war or been on the front lines of an attack to have PTSD. Often, PTSD can be hiding in your cells from a dysfunctional childhood or growing up in a home where your parents argued, even if you don't remember any particular incident. PTSD is the result of trauma hiding the real root cause of any condition or illness.

We are all born with only two fears: fear of falling, and fear of loud noises. All other fears are learned. As a result, an inborn fear can be triggered by raised voices, and become trauma; especially when they are those of your primary care givers: your Mom and Dad. Many children sit cowering under their blanket at night while parents are arguing downstairs unaware they can be heard. And, even if they cannot be heard, the mood in the home is significantly altered when there is dissension of any kind, and children pick it up the next day at breakfast.

If you have an abandonment issue of any kind, which can be physical: a parent leaving when you were too young to remember, divorce, separation, the death of a parent, one parent has to work long hours and is gone for significant periods of time. Or, it can be emotional: both parents are there but are not accessible emotionally, do not provide the affection, attention, and tenderness necessary for a child to thrive, you have trauma that has been hiding in the cells of your body that you may not even know is there. This trauma lies silently, until one day, much later, you start to get anxiety or panic attacks. At first, this anxiety might be triggered by a car accident, or sudden shock. But soon, one panic attack begets another. Or you might suddenly be hit by a wall of depression that causes you to either want to sleep most of the day and feel unmotivated to do anything you used to enjoy or be unable to sleep, resulting in chronic insomnia. You may begin to put on weight much later; excess weight is the result of feeling unsafe in some area of your life. The abandonment is at the root cause of the PTSD which in turn, causes certain unhealthy behavioral patterns.

Remember that this is not an exercise in blaming your parents for what happened in the past. Most parents do the best they can with what they had/knew at the time. Parents who were abusive were themselves abused and, although this is no excuse, they will pass it on if they believe that this kind of "discipline" was good for them or if they don't know any better.

There may be a tendency in you right now to deny that there was anything negative that happened in your childhood. Many people have assured me that they had a relatively happy upbringing, only to find out, at deeper assessment, that there was an incident, or that what appeared to be "normal" was really a dysfunctional familial environment.

Sometimes people will say, "Well I know I had a lousy childhood." But that alone is not an explanation that will help you to heal. Even knowing the trauma itself, may not help you to heal it. I am not in any way saying that parents are to blame. We are not engaging in an exercise to find fault with them. Anything that happened to you before age ten that was interpreted as bad can later on cause illness or dis ease, or sometimes, just a feeling of being incomplete or missing something. It does not have to be dramatic.

Laurie, a twenty-three-year-old, was having intense panic attacks and could not figure out what caused them. After taking her history, I could not find anything that could have been at the root cause of her anxiety, so I asked her if she wanted to do a regression. She agreed, and I gently took her back in time, not knowing where we would end up. Fortunately, Laurie trusted the process and really wanted to heal. So we went as far back as an incident that happened while she was still an infant in her crib. She remembered looking through the bars of her crib when she heard loud noises coming from her Mom as her Dad seemed to be trying to hurt her Mom.

Coming out of the regression, she was able to understand that witnessing her Mom and Dad making love, which she had misinterpreted as an act of aggression on the part of her Dad, was enough to cause the PTSD which later came out as panic or anxiety attacks, especially when she would start to get close to a man she liked. Again, processing the root cause alleviated the issue.

Knowing the root cause of your PTSD is not always enough to help you heal. You would have to allow yourself to understand some of the behavioral patterns that tend to come with PTSD:

1. Go back to your childhood and think about your friendships. Have you ever had a basic insecurity in any primary relationship going as far back as you can remember, which may be unconscious and may cause you to sabotage these relationships?

2. When you are in a good relationship, and you need to assert your boundaries as conflicts come up, do you hold the anger in, and later have unpredictable outbursts or have arguments with your mate which seem to be triggered by insignificant disagreements? Besides which, we never fight about what we think we're fighting about. It's always in some way, related to the past. (The root cause of cancer is anger held in [11] so it is never a good idea to ignore resentments and frustrations.)

3. Shutting down at times, emotionally and/or sexually and not knowing why.

4. The need for control because you had no control over the event that is at the root cause. However, when you try to control people or events and find that you can't, you may become overly controlling about your environment. Do you have a place for everything and everything in its place, but if someone dares to disturb this order of things, you get really upset? Do you check if the door is locked sixteen times?

5. Self-destructive behavior that can be some kind of addiction or obsession or becoming a workaholic or an overachiever. Do you find yourself driving through your local fast food place ordering two hamburgers, large fries, a milkshake and a dessert and eating all of it in your car, hiding from others? Do you smoke, use drugs (even excessive use of prescription medications) or alcohol?(12)

6. And any other dysfunctional behavior – you take your pick!

Start by being very gentle with yourself. Interrupt the judgment and maybe even the names you are calling yourself with the tool you already have: *Stop! Cancel! I am in charge of my life now!* Find the loving person that you can be and take yourself by the hand, one step at a time into relaxation by beginning with your deep breathing, and using the trigger word you chose earlier to begin to let go of your day.

Understanding where these patterns came from can help you to decide to process the root cause that has created havoc in your life. You can process it by putting yourself into a deep state of relaxation or hypnosis, and while you are in your safe place, take each negative event or trauma from the earliest to the latest, one by one, and turn each one from negative to positive, in your imagination. Go back in time and find the earliest memory of something negative that happened when you were a child. It could be falling off your bicycle or finding yourself alone when you get back from school. Take your time to do this thoroughly. Now imagine the perfect childhood you always wanted. Instead of witnessing Dad hitting Mom, Dad comes home, puts his arms around Mom, is affectionate with her.

You may have to do this one trauma at a time, if you have several. Take each negative memory one at a time and turn each one into a positive experience in your imagination. Be patient. This may take some time, visualizing the positive events you want to create until you feel good about them.

It may sound simplistic, but it works because the unconscious mind cannot tell the difference between what is really true and what is not, accepting your imaginative renderings as true, and automatically erasing all the negative tension around the event. We can change our past, no matter how bad it was, when we believe it's possible, by relaxing and using our imagination. It may take several times of doing this on your own for you to feel that you have changed your past.

In my healing center, I process the root cause neurologically which is a very powerful professional procedure. I do this in an hour's session and have successfully helped people to heal long-term PTSD. (See the testimonials at the beginning of this book.) This procedure cannot be done by yourself and requires professional training. Even a professional who has not been properly trained or who does not have long-term experience, can cause damage to the psyche.[6]

When you use your will power, you get resistance from your environment, from others, and even from yourself. Try telling yourself NOT to think of something specific. As an example tell yourself, "Don't think of the ice cream in the freezer, don't think of having another cigarette or another slice of cake or another portion of delicious food!" You would be thinking of the very thing you don't want to think about, until you would eventually succumb to doing what you know is not healthy for you. Remember, your unconscious mind takes every don't and turns it into a do!

On the other hand, if instead of using your will power you used your imagination, then nothing could oppose it. Your imagination is what you can use to create your new life, free of anything negative from the past. When you are in relaxation, in your safe place, and seeing and feeling your life the way you want it, and do this often enough, you will create what you see and feel. I know it sounds too easy or too good to be true, but if you don't give it a chance to work for you, how will you create something new and wonderful for yourself?

You can change anything you want to change by changing your belief systems. Everything begins with a thought. A thought becomes a feeling. A feeling becomes an emotion. An emotion becomes a belief, and that belief is the foundation for EVERYTHING that happens in your life! Events begin to happen to support that belief, and pretty soon, your life is off in a direction that feels out of your control.

Most people think, "I'll believe it when I see it." But the reality is, when you believe it, you will see it.(13).

Think of what happened in your early childhood that was either traumatic or negative for you. Now think of the beliefs you developed as a result of what happened. For example, Mom told you you were stupid out of her frustration. You heard, "I'm stupid. If Mom said so, it must be true." So then you go around looking at everything from the point of view of being stupid. "I can't do this." "I'm not good enough." "If they really knew me, they wouldn't like me." Etc.

As you continue with these beliefs, events happen around you to support them and you are on a downward roll. Look at every event that happened in your past that made those beliefs very true and you will understand that you created everything that happened in your life! This is quite a sobering thought. Nothing happens by accident. When we realize that we have created everything that has ever happened to us, we begin to be free of the past because we can create the kind of life we want by changing our beliefs.

Go back into your past and take the most scary thing that ever happened. Please trust that you will be able to not only overcome your greatest fear of feeling the feelings you felt back then, but that you will free yourself forever.

Go back to the most horrible memory you can think of, and allow yourself to feel all those scary feelings you experienced back then. This incident created negative beliefs for you, like, "I am scared. I am helpless. I am angry. I am alone. I am unwanted."

Now take three of these early negative beliefs, and think of the opposite of each one, and create a new affirmation: "I am intelligent. I am successful. I am powerful. I am lovable. I am worthy and deserving."

Take any three that resonate with you, and begin to repeat them to yourself. You might have to interrupt the resistance you begin to feel within you that keeps you from completing this exercise; but if you persist, you will reap the rewards of feeling healed.

You might have to use, "Stop! Cancel! I am in charge of my life now!", to interrupt the negative thoughts. Doing this as often as possible re-patterns your brain to become positive. Your brain is always responding to the fears within. So why not reset all your negative patterns by replacing them with new positive ones that make sense for you?

Marci was a fifteen-year-old student who was brought to my center by her Dad. She was having severe anxiety attacks and was cutting herself. When someone mutilates herself, it's usually because the emotional pain is too much to bear, so it's easier to feel physical pain. However, no one actually feels good about enduring physical pain either, and Marci expressed that she wanted to stop hurting herself. She had been cutting herself in inconspicuous places that she could hide beneath her clothes. She remembered that she had started to do this when she was being bullied at school two years before because she had formed a bond with another student, a boy, who was also being bullied. The boy, who was gay, killed himself. Marci felt responsible for his death, thinking that she had not stood up to the bullies.

I was able to get to the root cause of the anxiety attacks and the cutting, when Marci remembered the most painful time of her life when her parents had a terrible argument which led to their separation and a long custody battle over her.

Marci's three negative beliefs created out of this conflict were:

I am hurt. I am scared. I am alone.

After we processed the negative beliefs, she came up with:

I am happy. I am strong. I am lovable.

By the end of the three treatments, she left free of all anxiety and depression, had stopped cutting herself after the first treatment, and felt a strong sense of self-confidence. She called a few months later to tell me she had moved out of state to be with her Mom and sounded very happy.

If you find that it's getting too difficult for you to do this alone, I am always here to help. In my healing center, we do three treatments and people heal when they follow direction and use the tools. I process the root cause for you neurologically and physiologically; it is not the same processing described in this book because it would be impossible for you to do it for yourself.

Forgiveness removes only the untrue, lifting the shadows from the world and carrying it, safe and sure within its gentleness, to the bright world of new and clean perception. There is your purpose. And it is there that peace awaits you.

A Course in Miracles

CHAPTER FIVE

FORGIVENESS IS FREEDOM!

Most people have trouble forgiving the past and the people in their past. Forgiving yourself is even harder than forgiving others. So how do we forgive those who hurt us in the past? Forgiveness does not mean that you condone what happened or that you forget the past.

The next exercise is a process that works best if you are in your relaxed state in your own safe place as described in Chapter 3.

Once you have relaxed yourself and feel comfortable in your safe place, call out from within yourself that little child who is you. This child may appear at the age of your first negative incident or not. Usually the child who appears is ten years old or younger. Look closely at this child. You may see a longing or sadness in the eyes. First, admire the beauty of this child or the wholeness or the completeness: this child is perfect the way she/he is.

Tell this child that you are making contact because you are the adult now and only you can help her/him to heal from the past completely. If there was not enough attention from your parents, or enough demonstration of love, or enough tenderness, tell this child you will provide what was missing.

Now have this child stand facing you as you stand facing her/him, and look at her/his heart area. If you look carefully enough, you will see or sense a golden light hiding behind her/his heart. This is the presence of a Higher Self or Spirit or God or whatever you feel comfortable calling it. It is a presence and power for Good or Wisdom or Love that you know exists. Bring up that light so that it is illuminating that child from head to toe. Now, look down at your own heart and feel/sense that light that is within you and bring it out so that you feel that you are also illuminated from head to toe. Surround the two of you with this beautiful, protective light as you stand facing each other.

Silently send this child unconditional love from your heart to her/his heart, and notice that you are also receiving unconditional love from her/him. Take in the love, let it fill up your heart. And when you're ready, send unconditional forgiveness to this child: you are forgiving everything, everything this child has ever thought or said or done, and even what you think this child should have thought or said or done. You are forgiving yourself! When you're ready, say to this child, "I forgive you _____ (say the adult name of the child, your name), and I set you free." When you've said that, notice the countenance of the child. A smile may appear on her/his face or just a letting go. And you will feel a sense of calm and peace deep within yourself.

Promise this child that you will protect her/him from now on from toxic people, substances, places and events, as much as possible, and that you will bring her/him out again in your safe place at the last meditation of your day to have some good times or some fun times together. Now make this child very small, and place her back inside your heart where she /he belongs and where she/he will patiently wait for you to bring her out again.

Take a deep breath, and look way out in the distance as you continue to relax in your safe place. Notice a figure approaching from far away, perhaps waving to you, and as this figure approaches, you notice it's your Mom (or Dad first if you are a man). Have your Mom come up and stand in front of you. She will remain silent and open and receptive while she is here with you, even if that is not characteristic of her.

Tell your Mom (or Dad) whatever has been locked up in your heart that you may never have shared about your childhood, or anything else that you would like to share: your frustrations, fears, pain, as well as your joy and gratitude. At the end of all this sharing, ask your Mom for whatever it is that you need from her that will make you feel better.

Stand facing your Mom and find her golden light of Love and Wisdom in her heart, and bring out yours in your own heart. Then, surrounding the two of you with this protective light, silently send her unconditional love, and when you are ready, send her unconditional forgiveness. In this case, the forgiveness is for the woman who may have made mistakes. You may not necessarily need to forgive the words or actions from the past, but just the person. And say to her, "I forgive you, Mom, and I set you free." And gently release your Mom.

The purpose of forgiving everyone is so that you set yourself free from the past, remembering that whatever we give out to others we are giving to ourself, and vice-versa.

You do this again with your Dad (or Mom if you are a man) and release him with the words, "I forgive you, Dad, and I set you free." Do this also with others who may need your forgiveness or whose forgiveness you may need, those who are living and those who are on the other side.

When you have completed this forgiveness exercise, you will feel as though a weight has been lifted off you.

Lilly came to see me because she was obese and had trouble getting around. She was in her thirties and had a young daughter who was also overweight. She wanted to help her daughter to prevent her from becoming as obese as she was, and she also felt that it was time to release the weight she had gained over the years. As we spoke, I probed her childhood history. She broke down and told me that she had been "molested" repeatedly by her father over a period of years.

Eventually, at her second treatment, she opened up and described the rapes she had experienced by her father. It was not easy for her to get in touch with what had really happened, and although she was aware that she had put on so much weight to keep men literally away from her, she was having a hard time allowing me to process this root cause of all her physical problems. She tearfully told me she had never spoken about the rapes with anyone before. She also confided that she had left her husband as soon as she caught him inappropriately touching her daughter. Lilly did want to get over her painful past, and eventually allowed me to take her back to the most difficult memory so that I could process it neurologically. The processing helped her to turn her most negative beliefs into powerful, positive ones. The forgiveness exercise we did at the third treatment, helped her to release herself from her painful past and even to forgive and release her rapist!

At the completion of treatment, she left happy knowing that she was slowly, and safely releasing the weight that had kept her from becoming healthy and healed. She called occasionally to check in about her progress, and the last time we spoke, she had released over one hundred pounds and told me she was the happiest and healthiest she had ever been.

Love Is Letting Go Of Fear

Gerald G. Jampolsky

CHAPTER SIX

LETTING GO OF THE NEGATIVE EMOTIONS FROM THE PAST, PRESENT AND FUTURE

In order to let go of your negative emotions, it's important to first, own them. The primary negative emotions that I record with my clients are: anger, anxiety, depression, guilt, grief, stress, pain (physical and emotional). It helps to rate yourself on a scale of 0 to 10, the latter being the worst, over a specific period of time such as: in the last six months, rate yourself on your level of expressed anger and/or held-in anger. (SUDS: subjective units of distress scale)

Then, rate yourself before you started doing all this work and now, after beginning this work. When I'm working with people, I ask them to evaluate themselves at the beginning and at the end of each session so that they can actually notice their own improvement. At the last session, which is the third treatment, I help them to process their emotions from the past, present, and future (whatever level they are now at) by taking them through a specific visualization.

You can do an adaptation of this process by first visualizing time however it occurs to you as a line or continuum from present to now to future either in front of you from left to right or stretching from behind you to infinity in front of you, or however you picture time.(14) Then picture yourself floating above this line to sometime in the past, facing the past, when each of these negative emotions were at their highest. Now, turn around, and face the future, remaining just before that negative emotion took place on your line. As you do this, you'll notice that you can no longer feel the emotion. It's just gone. Then, if you allow yourself to do this with each emotion, it will also be gone, so that if you go back to test if you feel them in the past, they're all gone, and if you test if you can feel them in the future, they're also all gone.

When you rate yourself on the scales for each of the negative emotions, at the end of this process, you will find that you have brought them down to zero or close to zero. It is easier for the client when I do this for them and help them get through it. After processing the negative emotions, I usually ask the client to stand in the now, turn towards the past, and if there are any dark areas on their line, I ask them to clear it up with the powerful white light from above. We do the same thing with the future.

Michelle was in her late fifties and had gone back home to live with her Mom because she was so anxious and depressed and was in a constant state of self-criticism and complaint. She decided to come to see me after having spent time in the hospital, and noticing that even with the anti-depressants and sleep medications she was given, she was not improving. She claimed that one of the doctors had scared her to death by giving her a life-threatening diagnosis.

She rated herself at the top of the scale for every negative emotion. As I began to work with her, her resistance was so great, that she would interrupt the work I would be doing with her just at the moment she would begin to relax and let go. The more she would interrupt, the more anxious she became. I would calm her down, and as soon as I would begin to empower her with tools, she would jump up and refuse to allow me to continue. I had to resort to an indirect way of working with her and to give her a choice of different tools she could use.

When she realized that she could begin to trust me, she stopped fighting me, let go of the need to control, and allowed me to work with her. The ratings on her scales for the negative emotions, including anxiety and depression began to come down.

She also began to work with a physician who thoroughly tested her for every possible condition, and told her that all her tests showed that she was healthy.

After our work together, Michelle was able to return to her own home, and told me a story about what happened to her as she was on her way home. She had been doing her visualizations of her most desired goal, seeing her goal accomplished, and by the time she reached her home, there was her most desired outcome right in front of her! She could see that as soon as she stopped using her tools, she would be out of control again but she realized that when she would stay centered and focused on the present moment, she could let go and relax. When she tried to use her will power, her life would reflect chaos, but when she allowed her imagination to work in a positive way, there was no opposition to what she could create.

There are only two ways to live your life.
One is as though nothing is a miracle.
The other is as though everything is.

Albert Einstein

CHAPTER SEVEN

SETTING YOUR GOALS FOR THE FUTURE

Now see yourself having accomplished all your goals, being happy and healthy and healed and prosperous or successful, and set a date for this to be true and release this into that date. By doing this releasing to the unconscious mind or to your Higher Power, you are surrendering the need to control your future. In doing that, you are no longer concerned about making it happen or using your will power or forcing something to happen. The outcome is usually much more magnificent than you could ever have imagined it.

Your body is always talking to you, giving you feedback about your life. It is very literal. If you meditate or become very mindful of what your body is telling you, you will know how to help yourself heal. For example, if I have arthritis in my hands, and I have pain in my hands, I would first ask myself: what is going on in my life that I can't handle? What am I being rigid about in my life? And I would make a list and rate myself on the level of pain. Then I would do everything outlined from the beginning of this book and rate myself again and notice that the pain is gone because of all the work I have done. I could also even visualize my fingers straightening up and the swelling diminishing. This, along with a mindful change in my daily nutrition, would be helpful in re-establishing my complete health.

We are all co-creators in our life. If we believe that life just happens, then we don't have the freedom to create our destiny. I believe that nothing happens by accident, that all fear can be transformed by my faith, and that I am in charge of everything I manifest in my life, good and bad.

My grandmother believed she was blessed (and her name was Fortunee which means fortunate) even though she experienced great loss in her life, including losing a son in his early twenties. Because of her belief system, she was always able to surmount great obstacles and remain optimistic no matter how dark her life seemed to be to the outsider.

The point is that we can choose to live in the darkness or in the light, we choose our mood at any given time, and we create either our deepest fears or our greatest miracles through every thought we think, every word we utter, and every action we undertake.

Having studied theology and most of the great religions in the world, and having experienced living in many different cultures, I have come to the realization that we choose our destiny right from the beginning, we choose our sacred contracts with all the people who are meant to enter our life, and we choose the circumstances in detail. Then, we are born and forget all that. However, the circumstances in our life awaken us to the memories deep within our spirit that we chose our parents and all the ones who have come in since, for a purpose. If we learn that lesson, then we move onto the next one at a higher level of evolution. If we do not learn that lesson, whatever it might be for each one of us, then the lesson presents itself in a more evident, and often, more difficult way.

Your lessons are opportunities to retrace the steps that lead you to your bliss which is deep inside you. It is your inner core whether you acknowledge it or not. You may call it "God within", or "Christ Consciousness", or "Higher Self", or "Holy Spirit" or "Buddha Nature". That is the same consciousness within also accessed through the unconscious mind. When you decide to take this journey within to find the light or the holy grail, or your true Self, you will have to get through the heart of darkness, your own fundamental darkness, before you can come out to the brilliant, pure, pristine light of understanding or what is often termed as "Enlightenment".

The darkness that exists within each of us is the negativity or shadow beliefs that are hidden from our conscious self. This is the part within that speaks all the negative beliefs, such as, "Who am I kidding? I am not enough. I'll never be able to do that!" etc.

The meditative state you go into every day helps you to train your body-mind-spirit to go into deep relaxation, over and over again. When you are in that alpha state of relaxation, you undo the negative voice within. After going into relaxation training over a certain period of time, you will begin to live more intuitively, and you will realize that every time you have trusted your intuition, you were brought to wherever you needed to be at the right time. You may begin to notice that your intuition is getting stronger and that positive coincidences are becoming the rule rather than the exception in your life.

I was blessed with the ability to communicate with my Spirit Guides at a very young age but stopped deliberately spending time with them when I noticed that none of my friends did, and that they thought I was weird. At the time, I wanted to fit in, so I gave up living in the other dimension. It was only much later, when I started to do assiduous daily meditation that I began to tap into that "gift" again, was able to go into spontaneous regressions into the past which showed me the lessons I needed to learn, that I allowed myself to live consciously again.

I was able to find happiness deep within myself, even during difficult times which seemed to threaten my ability to find any peace. And if I could do it, I know that you can too! Remember to be kind and gentle with yourself, and if you need extra help, there is no shame in reaching out – I am here for you.

Everyone has this "gift" within. When you understand that there are no accidents, and that you chose every little thing that has ever happened, you will begin to notice the opportunities for you to grow and learn in a new and spiritual way. When you take responsibility for your life, you experience the freedom to choose to be who you were really meant to be. You will find that the journey begins in your mind and ends up in your heart. Then, you will know that your true purpose in life – your higher purpose is to be of service.

You can choose to use this gift so that you can find out firsthand, that you are more than the body you are inhabiting right now. That no matter how many obstacles have come into your life, they are your true friends. Embrace them, and accept them for what they bring you. Eventually, you will have no more fears, for you will know, with complete confidence that when your body is no more, your spirit will continue to live on in what is known as Ultimate Reality where you will continue to manifest your highest purpose of being of service to God and to others.

Be grateful for your body which has been the steppingstone to your Spirit, and, in the meantime, while you continue to evolve and to live consciously, enjoy every single moment of your life, be grateful even for your obstacles for they will show you the way to the light every time, reminding you that you are more than your body!

NOTES AND BIBLIOGRAPHY

1. Carson, Viviane. ***Kindred Spirits, A Double Memoir.*** California: work in progress.

2. Goleman, Daniel. ***Emotional Intelligence.*** New York: Bantam Books, 1995.

3. Carson, Viviane. ***Dr. Carson's Alternative Health Care Center.*** Website: http://www.drvcarson.com/ Who We Are. Copyright 2002.

4. Ibid.

5. Pert, Candace. ***Molecules of Emotion.*** New York: Scribner, 1997.

6. Shapiro, Francine. ***Eye Movement Desensitization and Reprocessing.*** New York: The Guilford Press, 1995.

7. Hicks, Esther and Jerry. ***Ask and It Is Given.*** California: Hay House, Inc., 2004.

8. Bandler, Richard, and Grinder, John. ***Reframing.*** Utah: Real People Press, 1982.

9. Hawkins, David R. ***Power vs. Force.*** California: Hay House, Inc., 1995.

10. Chopra, Deepak. ***Quantum Healing.*** New York: Bantam Books, 1990.

11. Hay, Louise L. ***You Can Heal Your Life.*** California: Hay House, Inc., 1999.

12. Anderson, Susan. T***he Journey from Abandonment to Healing.*** New York: The Berkley Publishing Group, 2000.

13. Dyer, Wayne. ***You'll See It When You Believe It.*** New York: Harper Collins Publishers, Inc., 1989.

14. James, Tad, and Woodsmall, Wyatt. ***Time Line Therapy and The Basis of Personality.*** California: Meta Publications, In., 1988.

Every day in every way
I am getting better and better.

Émile Coué

Acknowledgments

I would like to thank Bill Wisner for his encouragement to write this book. He never gave up on me, even when I felt I was lost.

I would like to acknowledge all the people whose work, and in many cases, whose help was significant in inspiring me to develop my healing method:

Louise Hay, Marianne Williamson, Caroline Myss, Émile Coué, Ernest Holmes, Dr. Krasner, Tad James, Daniel Goleman, Pete Sanders, Susan Anderson, Joseph Murphy, and Francine Shapiro.

I would like to give thanks to those who personally assisted me in completing this book:

Donna Kozik who got me started.

Holly Newlon who made two good suggestions.

My Mom, Marcelle whose spirit infuses all my work.

My Dad, Germain, whose gentle memory always reminds me to be kind.

My two Grandmothers, Fortunée and Perline who opened the path to wisdom for me.

And lastly, tremendous gratitude for my daily, assiduous meditation practice which lit my journey through all the lows and highs of the last 35 years. This powerful meditation inspires me to continue to evolve every day of my life and to offer a hand to all those who reach out.

Love is the most powerful force in the Universe.